# Change Your
# Marketing
# Change Your
# Results

## How to get ma$$ive results from marketing at your financial institution.

## Jay Kassing

MARQUIS Press

MARQUIS Press

Change Your Marketing Change Your Results: *How to get ma$$ive results from marketing at your financial institution.*

Design and Production by Charles Flemming – info@cflemming.com

ISBN 978-0615464688

Books are made available by MARQUIS Press in special quantity discounts. Please contact the publisher at:

MARQUIS Press
5212 Tennyson Pkwy. #150
Plano, TX 75024

> ## "A man travels the world over in search of what he needs and returns home to find it."
>
> ### — George Moore

**To my bride and our five short people...**

Thank you for making a home and a life where my heart longs to be.

**To Mom and Dad...**

Much of what I am begins with the example you set.

Your expectations of me (and the other four) established a quiet purpose.

I hope that Jennifer and I can impart that same result in our children.

# Table of Contents:

# Does your marketing stink?

## Maybe. Maybe not.

# Want a quick smell test?

# Does your marketing team measure the results of their marketing activities?

No? *"Shhh, I smell something."*

Explore the following pages. Likely you and your institution have the right overall philosophy…you just haven't leveraged your marketing to drive profitable growth that benefits your income statement, if not your balance sheet.

## Leverage Marketing

# In a recent survey of financial institutions, we discovered two compelling pieces of information.

# ( 1 )

**37%** of financial institutions expect their marketing team to measure the impact of their marketing.

# ( 2 )

**75%** of these banks and credit unions had a member of marketing on their executive management team.

# So...

**75%** of Marketers who prove their ROI are members of the senior management team.

Is this a coincidence?

Not likely.

"Facts are stubborn things; and whatever may be our wishes, our inclinations, or the dictates of our passion, they cannot alter the state of facts and evidence."

— John Adams

# What could be wrong with how you are doing marketing today?

Besides having a general lack of accountability related to performance measurement in marketing, most financial institutions have simply focused their marketing staff on non-growth-related activities.

# Measuring your marketing will do more for your growth than high definition has done for TV.

# Massive profit growth will not happen without a dramatic paradigm shift in what you expect from your marketing.

# Focus on client retention

Another recent study* proved that the average financial institution loses 14.6% of their clients annually. Yes. That means every year. Said another way, you will have to replace the profit generated from the clients you lose each year, before you can grow revenue just one dollar.

And remember, 14.6% is an average. If you have not made retention a priority, your attrition rate could be much worse. Establishing an effective retention program is one area where your marketing can make a significant difference.

*Celent Communications

# Unite the goals of Marketing & Sales

In theory, everyone believes that their marketing and sales teams have joined forces, like super heroes fighting evil. In reality, it is rarely true. Strategically, you know where you need to go. Why isn't your marketing team focused on generating leads for your sales staff that fit your "strategic" expectations?

Sadly, the answer is…*inertia*. Marketing and sales folks simply fall into the same old habits. Phrases like, "This is how we have always done it" abound. To get your teams to stop "working in silos," they have to break the habit.

## Getting sales and marketing in alignment is vital for massive growth.

# The Math of Growth.

**Growth doesn't just "*happen*." Can aligning marketing and sales make a difference? Everyone say it together... "*Show me the Algebra!*" The following formula clearly outlines why...**

## [ a ]

Marketing and sales must be on the same page, and

## [ b ]

Marketing is a major player in the growth of your financial institution.

$$\int \frac{dx}{x^n(x^n+a^n)} = \frac{1}{a^n}\int \frac{dx}{x^m(x^n-} $$

$$\int \frac{dx}{\sqrt{x^n+a^n}} = \frac{1}{n\sqrt{a^n}}\ln\int \frac{\sqrt{x^n-}}{\sqrt{x^n+}}$$

$$\int \frac{dx}{x^m(x^n-a^n)^r} = \frac{1}{a^n}\int \frac{dx}{x^{m-n}(} $$

$$\int \frac{dx}{x\sqrt{x^n-a^n}} = \frac{2}{n\sqrt{a^n}}\cos$$

$$\int \frac{dx}{} = \frac{1}{} $$

# The basic equation for business growth.

*The following is a basic growth equation for every financial institution (and you said you would never use Algebra…)*

Growth = (# of opportunities X closing ratio) – attrition rate.

This math equation simply says that growth is a product of the number of new sales opportunities (which obviously come from a variety of marketing sources) that are closed by your sales staff, subtracting the profit and revenue lost from clients who leave.

Because we have defined the "growth" equation above, shouldn't we add a number we want for growth? Sure. Let's say our goal is 10% overall growth.

10% Growth =

(# of opportunities × closing ratio)

– attrition rate

# Before we cover the elements inside the parentheses, let's discuss the last component, attrition rate.

While we have seen more than just a couple banks and credit unions that are losing more than 20% of their clients every year, it has been reasonably established that the average institution loses 15%. **Just think about how hard it is to grow, when you have to replace 15% of your overall client base, before you can grow even one dollar.**

Can you grow 10% without reducing your attrition? Yes, but that puts even greater stress on your marketing and sales staffs to both work together and seriously amp up the results. The average attrition rate for financial institutions is just under 15%. This number excludes the fact that your institution's assets (loans) are also paying down over the course of the year, and those need to be replaced as well! Let's add the average attrition rate to our equation.

$$10\% \text{ Growth} =$$
$$(\# \text{ of opportunities} \times \text{closing ratio})$$
$$- 15\% \text{ attrition rate}$$

## Inside the parentheses is where most institutions do their work.

But how are most institutions generating qualified leads and how do they amp up that number enough to move the needle? And is the sales organization efficiently and effectively closing that business? Unfortunately for many organizations, marketing and sales aren't working together. Marketing does their thing. The sales team does theirs.

Can you get 10% more leads and maybe a 10% higher closing rate? Will that be enough if you lose 15% through attrition? You need to get more leads. And that must be a marketing function, not a directive for your sales team to make more cold calls.

$$10\% \text{ Growth} =$$
$$(\text{Opportunities grow} > 10\%$$
$$\times \text{ closing ratio} > 10\% \text{ better})$$
$$- 15\% \text{ attrition rate}$$

# Is the reality of this growth equation scary?

**It shouldn't be.** Yet, massive profit growth is the result of having leveraged marketing to deliver more sales opportunities and to reduce attrition. Sales has a part to play here, as always.

Fairy tales are more than true — not because they tell us dragons exist, but because they tell us dragons can be beaten.

— G. K. Chesterton

# Are you prepared to slay the dragon that is "the inertia of how you currently employ marketing?"

"Insanity: doing the same thing over and over again and expecting different results."

— Albert Einstein

# But it may not be marketing's fault.

## Are they being asked to do the wrong things?

Do members of the Board of Directors, the CFO, CEO or anyone else in senior management view marketing as a "cost" of doing business or as a necessary evil? Shouldn't we start with the idea that marketing is the *directly measurable* reason why growth happens?

**Marketing** must talk about and take action on the same things **Management** cares about.

- Value Creation & Profitable Growth

- Interest Spread Management & Preservation

- Loyalty/Franchise Building
  (the single most important determinant of profitability)

**How does your Marketing team prove to you that what they do with their budget dollars actually helps to achieve these goals?**

"The only measure
of what you believe
is what you do."

— Ashley Montagu

# Think differently.

# What must happen for your institution to get massive profit growth?

- Marketing must be a partner in driving growth.

- Marketing must be *aligned* with Sales.

- Marketing must get, use, and be the source of reliable business intelligence and knowledge.

- Marketing must identify which relationships deliver the profit.

- Marketing must address Client Attrition and build client retention/loyalty.

- Marketing must be *measurable*.

- Marketing must generate qualified leads for the sales team.

# Marketing must be a partner in driving growth.

## Every institution seeks growth.

It is vitally important to understand how difficult it is to grow your institution's ROE/ROA, year over year. Unfortunately, the math works in such a way that the more success you have, the harder it is to repeat the success.

**This underscores the need to get your marketing to work for you in a big way.**

# What if Sales and Marketing were aligned?

Across 315 enterprises, The CMO Council and Aberdeen Research found "When Sales and Marketing are truly aligned, revenues grow 50% year after year on 21% higher sales conversions." Imagine what might happen if your sales and marketing teams worked together!

"To succeed as a team is to hold all of the members accountable for their expertise".

— Mitchell Caplan

---

"The greatest obstacle to discovery is not ignorance—it is the illusion of knowledge."

— Daniel J. Boorstin

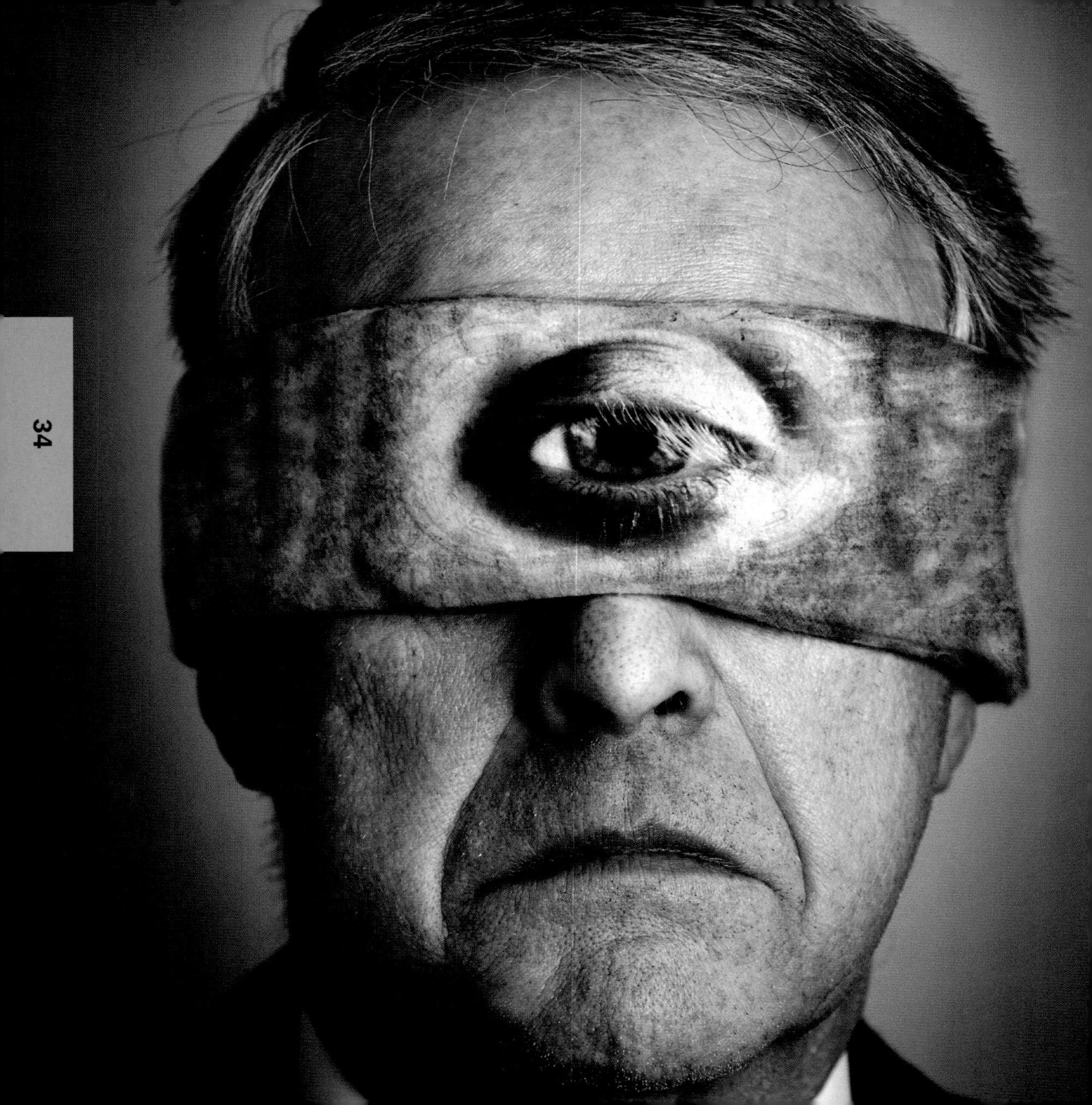

# Does anyone doubt that information is power?

Sir Francis Bacon once said, "Knowledge is power," which is the same thing contextually. Information gives us knowledge. And **knowledge is power***...in the hands of someone who understands what it means and what to do with it.* No one could say with a straight face that they would rather rely on ignorance. Certainly no leader would.

"It is no good to try to stop knowledge from going forward. Ignorance is never better than knowledge."

— Enrico Fermi

"We can have facts without thinking but we cannot have thinking without facts."

— John Dewey

"All men by nature desire knowledge."

— Aristotle

---

"To be conscious that you are ignorant is a great step to knowledge."

— Benjamin Disraeli

# Are you still in the dark ages, as it relates to business intelligence?

## History: You can change with it... or be changed by it.

Through time we have essentially progressed from the Stone Age, to the Bronze Age, to the Industrial Age, on to the Age of Administration, to the Computer Age, through to the Information Age.

Today, we can all simply "Google" to get most everything we want. But Google doesn't provide intelligence, only data. In the same way, your core system has tons of data about all of your accounts, yet it can't analyze anything or provide business intelligence. To get information that you can act upon, marketers and management need the tools that provide them this knowledge.

# "Facts do not cease to exist because they are ignored."

— Aldous Huxley

# Marketing must get, use, and be the source of reliable business intelligence and knowledge.

## It is an MCIF software program that provides this market and client intelligence.

Much of the information you seek to know and learn about your existing book of business is driven by having and using an MCIF (Marketing Central Information File). Historically, these software products have been managed by Marketing.

Ironically, many in Marketing do not fully appreciate that they have the keys to the information kingdom.

# 87% of the top performing institutions in the country have an MCIF. That said, why do less than 10% of all other financial institutions have one?

While most institutions you compete with lack true business intelligence, once you have and harness the power of information – you will have a significant competitive advantage.

"The kind of data available to the great company and good one is about the same. The difference is the great company will turn the data they do have – into information they cannot ignore." —Jim Collins, *Good to Great*

# MCIF is uniquely a noun and a verb.

It is a noun because an MCIF is the place where you can bring all of your institution's independent data silos (accounts) into one database. Once you have collected all of the data—the MCIF becomes a verb— inspiring action! All the cool action words, like *analyze*, *segment*, *campaign management*, *mapping*, etc., are included…and especially *measurement*!

You need to do the same. What information will you uncover that cannot be ignored? Then, armed with these compelling facts, you need to reach out to clients and prospects alike in ways that can be measured. Massive growth will follow.

"All truths are easy to understand once they are discovered; the point is to discover them."

— Galileo Galilei

# 5 of the 7 keys

to massive growth in marketing at financial institutions rely on the use of an MCIF software program.

**Can you afford not to have one,** especially if you want ma$$ive profit growth?

# Sobering facts about Retention.

## 60% – 80%

...of customers who defect to a competitor said they were satisfied or very satisfied on the survey just prior to their defection (Bain & Co. research).

## 85%

...of an organization's customers claim to be "satisfied," but still show a willingness to wander away to another provider (Prof. Robert Peterson, Univ. of Texas).

Other research shows that a customer's future intentions are not as closely related to satisfactions as they are to the relationship, or emotional connection, with the institution (ABA Bank Marketing Magazine, October 2010).

# There is no "WOW!" in satisfied.

## There is no *loyalty* in it, either.

# Marketing must identify which relationships deliver the profit.

Would it surprise you to know that only a few hundred of your existing relationships deliver all the bottom-line profit for your institution? It's true. After studying hundreds of financial institutions' data…we found that the profit generated by just the Top 1% of the relationships (at most financial institutions) equals about 100% of their profit.

Don't you need to know which of your client relationships bring you your profit? In the end, whether your institution's profit is derived from your Top 1% or your Top 4%, the important thing is to know who they are.

**If only 200-300 of your client relationships delivered all your institution's profit…what would you do with this knowledge? Get Marketing on that!**

# Forget 80:20. Meet the 100:1 rule.

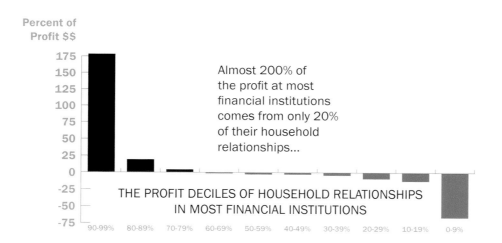

Percent of Profit $$

Almost 200% of the profit at most financial institutions comes from only 20% of their household relationships...

THE PROFIT DECILES OF HOUSEHOLD RELATIONSHIPS
IN MOST FINANCIAL INSTITUTIONS

90-99%  80-89%  70-79%  60-69%  50-59%  40-49%  30-39%  20-29%  10-19%  0-9%

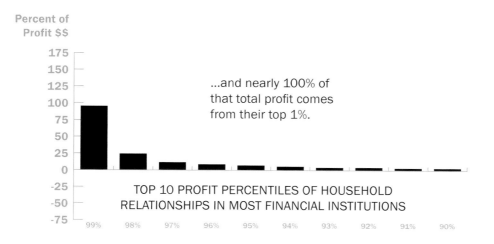

Percent of Profit $$

...and nearly 100% of that total profit comes from their top 1%.

TOP 10 PROFIT PERCENTILES OF HOUSEHOLD
RELATIONSHIPS IN MOST FINANCIAL INSTITUTIONS

99%  98%  97%  96%  95%  94%  93%  92%  91%  90%

# Are your best clients leaving you?

## Research says yes.

In fact, your best clients are leaving at just about the same rate as your other clients. That means that your high-value relationships and the profit they provide are leaving. Why? You must find out not only why, but Who? Then you need to focus on retaining your high-profit relationships.

"It's not enough
that we do our best;
sometimes we have to
do what's required."

— Sir Winston Churchill

# What would happen if you improved your overall retention rate by 1%?

According to Frederich Reichheld from his book, *The Loyalty Effect*, a 1% increase in overall client retention will add 17% to your bottom line. **Amazing research**. Read the book. Better still, get in the retention business.

Unfortunately, you and your peers have neglected retention to your own detriment. Like water seeping from the bottom of a leaky bucket, you pour eight new accounts each week into the bucket only to have seven seep out. This makes it frustratingly difficult to grow, and it underscores why retention is so critical.

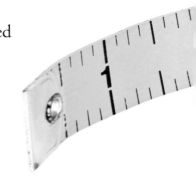

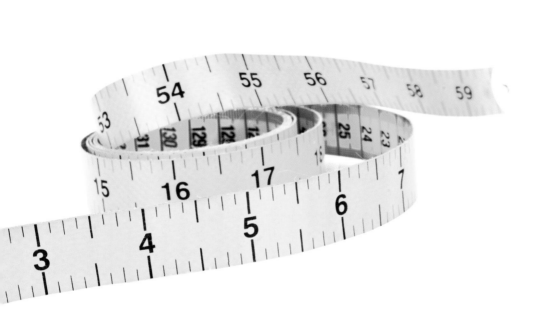

# Marketing must be Measurable.

Are you measuring your marketing activities now? So much of what many in marketing have been doing, isn't measured.

No wonder "marketing" is often the first place senior management looks to make budget cuts. Without proof of any results, marketing becomes less relevant, and less vital.

# What is difficult to measure?

**Advertising.** Whether the buys are for cable TV, newspaper or radio, the ability to measure the impact of these investments is limited. That doesn't necessarily rule out these activities, but they should become a smaller part of the overall marketing budget. It can no longer swallow up half the marketing budget. It is okay to create a brand position for your institution by using advertising, but don't expect a lot of foot traffic as a result.

**PR.** The amount of money that most institutions dedicate to fund local PR projects has nominal present or future value. Sure there is some local "community spirit" value, some benefit for supporting your Community Reinvestment Act (CRA) program, and clearly some good comes from using PR dollars to support the non-profit activities your large clients (whom you wish to retain) are into... but without a plan, much of it is wasted.

# What is *easy* to measure?

**Direct marketing.** This can take the form of direct mail, email marketing and web activities. All of these elements are directly measurable.

Instead of living with the same old marketing that provides nominal measurable proof of ROI, direct marketing activities can help your organization measurably grow. And marketing will deliver proof of this growth by directly measuring the ROI of these campaigns. This philosophical shift will turn your marketing department from a "cost center" into a revenue generating engine for growth.

Reach your individual clients with specific offers that are relevant to them personally. This begins by having a data-driven marketing plan. And this plan starts with having MCIF business intelligence.

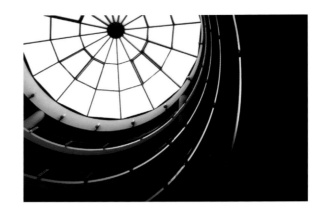

# Direct marketing is highly targeted and extremely measurable.

Dollar for dollar, direct marketing is the best method to drive your message and generate qualified leads on the products you want to sell. At least half of your marketing budget should be spent on direct marketing, in alignment with your strategic sales objectives.

**There is nothing else a financial institution can do to market themselves to new prospects or existing clients that will provide the meaningful ROI that direct marketing can.**

# Client intelligence drives ROI in marketing!

# There is even more power in direct marketing when you employ variable data.

Variable data doesn't simply mean mail merge in the client's name and address. Besides the name, personalize the mail/email piece to include the unique product offer, a picture that is pleasing to your client (think demographically), the nearest branch location, the specific branch contact, the signature of that officer and even a picture of the officer to call.

All of these variable data elements are easy to include in direct marketing and have a giant impact on response rates and ROI.

## Get results with one-to-one marketing using variable data with your direct marketing!

# "Things do not change; we change."

— Henry David Thoreau

# Marketing must generate qualified leads for the sales team.

## Direct marketing is great for generating leads for your branches and sales teams.

The primary objective for marketing, if you are to get massive profit growth, is for them to use the client intelligence provided by an MCIF to find sales opportunities that mirror your strategic sales goals.

## Marketing can do this?

## Yes...they already are at most high-performing financial institutions. Have any of your competitors already figured this out?

# Track the leads you do get.

Let's assume for the moment (but you better not) that marketing has generated leads from a direct marketing campaign. How are you tracking the responses that come into a branch? Please don't say that you aren't. This is essential feedback for marketers.

If 1,000 pieces of mail were sent to your clients, and 80 responded, marketing needs to know. They are the lead generators, not the sales people.

How many sales resulted from these 80 leads? Let's say you closed 20 of them. That represents a 25% closing ratio. Understanding this ratio may in itself provide good talking points for coaching your sales team. Is a 25% closing ratio good? If sales and marketing are aligned, they can work together to get higher response rates and a better closing ratio.

## Automate your lead and referral tracking.

# Marketing & Sales need immediate feedback on who, what, when, and the status of every lead, lost sale, and closed sales lead.

Why? Because you should measure all marketing activity. And because marketing and sales are aligned, their joint activity should be measured also. By the way, if you have automated your referrals and pay incentives based upon them…it will be dramatically easier for your HR folks to track and measure performance to calculate incentives.

# If it isn't measured, it didn't happen.

# Do you have a Unique Selling Proposition?

Financial services aren't exactly sexy products. And considering that research has proven that consumers feel that "if you have seen one financial institution, you have seen them all," how do you stand above what your peers provide? What makes how you deliver the "same old products" different?

If you can wrestle this concept to the ground, you will have a distinct and sustainable sales and marketing advantage over everyone else in your market. Hint: Don't say it is "customer service." Every financial institution thinks that is their edge. *It is almost always* **not** *customer service.*

# Why is it vital to cross-sell existing relationships?

**It is 8 to 10 times less expensive to cross-sell your existing client something else, than it is to reach out to someone that has never done business with you.**

If you aren't spending your limited marketing dollars cross-selling your existing clients something else, then you are bungling your most affordable growth opportunity. Oh, and by the way, besides being less expensive to sell…your existing clients are also 8-10 times more likely to buy something else than a new prospect would be.

Kind of makes you feel silly for always trying to get new accounts from brand new relationships first, when cross-selling is the best first strategy, doesn't it?

# How many of your client relationships only have one account with you?

Would it surprise you to learn around 40% of your clients have one lonely account with your institution? This is a high-risk area from a retention standpoint. It can also serve as a target-rich cross-selling segment for you.

Statistically speaking, half of these folks will leave you, if not now… soon. Cross-sell them something else and their risk of leaving you is reduced dramatically. You spent lavishly to obtain these clients. Keeping clients (who already trust you at least enough to have one product with you) is always good business and they are a great deal easier to sell than chasing new relationships.

# 40% :

the percentage of clients
who only have one account
at your institution...

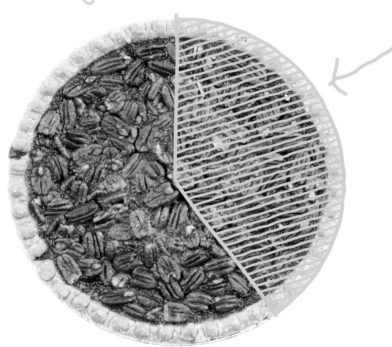

"...awfully close to half, isn't it?"

# Onboarding your way to cross-sales success!

## What is Onboarding and why should you care?

Did you know that your new relationships are dramatically more likely to buy something else from you during the 30-180 days after first opening that account, than at any other time? **In fact, 80% of cross-sales occur during this initial time frame.** But you have to ask them for more business.

What if you sent specific offers (via direct mail/email) to every new client relationship? What if you did it every month for half a year? This is Onboarding. What if each product or service you offered was specifically chosen to fit the needs of each new client, employing the variable data we discussed earlier? Set up properly, your Onboarding program will generate cross-sales at **better than a 10% response rate**.

## Get measurable growth with Onboarding!

## Results with Onboarding.

There is, without question, provable and meaningful revenue and profit enhancement available from Onboarding. Ask your marketing team if they are doing it. If they aren't, ask "Why not?"

We have seen financial institutions generate millions of dollars from this marketing technique alone. And the beauty is that Onboarding helps you not only to generate awesome growth, but it helps you to improve retention rates—at the same time.

# Growth isn't always easy, but it doesn't have to be hard, either.

# Why is Market Share and Share of Wallet information important?

For the sake of not leaving something unsaid, it is vital for you to know the share of market you own, if for nothing else than to validate that you are who you think you are. In the same way, think of the opportunities that will open up by knowing how much more business there is available from your own clients…or the market as a whole.

Marketing today requires that you strategically understand how you need to attack the market. Only real knowledge about your market share and share of wallet gives you this ability.

# Pricing Products for Profit.

When you see almost one thousand different financial institutions' data, you find some crazy things. Would you be surprised to know that over 70% of the products being sold by financial institutions are below their costs? Crazy, huh? Are you doing the same thing?

You need to review your product pricing strategy, especially now that some fee-generating activities have been taken away.

If your marketing folks have a real understanding of how your institution makes money, they will be reluctant to price your products underwater, or create balance sheet issues.

And as long as we're doing math – your marketing team needs to concentrate on adding products at a balance that makes them profitable.

# Budgeting for Success

Most organizations budget for marketing in two ways: Some institutions use the "let's give marketing X% more than last year's budget, that will pacify them" method; others are fond of the straight math option in the "one tenth, of one percent of total assets" method. Both methods are simple, but neither appears to be strategic. Shouldn't your marketing budget be based upon the growth goals you wish to achieve?

## What activities afford marketing the best opportunity to deliver ROI and growth?

## Budget for those.

# Allocating the Budget.

Start with this general budget allocation, and adjust accordingly to achieve **your stated goals**.

| | | |
|---|---|---|
| Advertising | 20% | $ 40,000 |
| Special Events | 7.5% | $ 15,000 |
| Literature, etc. | 2.5% | $ 5,000 |
| PR | 20% | $ 40,000 |
| Direct Marketing | 50% | $ 100,000 |
| | | |
| Total Marketing Budget | 100% | $ 200,000 |

## Budget most for the activities that deliver you measurable results.

# Your marketing team must understand how your financial institution makes money.

Marketers must move beyond "fonts and colors." Professional marketers need to be fundamentally aware of how their actions will impact the bottom line. Ideally, someone on your marketing staff must be active on your asset liability committee.

**Profitability is like sausage; everyone loves to eat it, but no one wants to know how it is made.**

# A new way to manage PR?

We have seen a number of institutions adopt strict rules for what causes PR dollars can be used. In other words, develop a corporate giving statement that outlines what types of activities you will support. Something like: "Our bank supports children's programs in our community." If the PR request doesn't support this cause, they don't get any money.

Be clear and upfront about your rules and overarching PR goals with your community and it will both narrow to whom you give money (and maybe provide support in a more meaningful way), but will also reduce the number of requests. And in the end, all of the PR money you have budgeted will go to causes near and dear to the heart of what your institution is all about.

"It is not who is right, but what is right, that is of importance."

— Thomas Henry Huxley

# Build an incentive plan for growth.

If you want growth, incent it. Sadly, many financial institutions are paying out loads of cash for nothing. Aren't incentives supposed to reward better results? Why then pay for results that will happen without incentives?

Regain some sanity in your incentive plan. Determine the run-rate of new account activity before you establish any incentive schedule. Once you know that you always get 10 new checking accounts per month from the West Branch, only pay incentives on activity above this baseline level. In other words, don't pay for the first 10 accounts; pay even better incentives on every account over ten!

*Style* is more important than *stuff* to the clients who want to be in control.

# Embrace Email Marketing

All of the benefits of direct mail can be derived from using email marketing. Highly targeted. One-to-One message. Measurable response rates. Provable ROI. And, email marketing is even less expensive than its sister technique, direct mail. Combining email with direct mail in a multi-channel marketing effort is a surefire way to generate growth.

# Personal URLs (PURLs)

PURLs are micro web sites designed to give the receiver of direct mail the means to move to an online, interactive and individual experience. Each piece of mail is printed with a personal web address for your clients and prospects (theirname.webaddress.com). The user enters that address into his browser and instantly personal, relevant content is provided. PURLS are used to provide incentives (cash or merchandise to open a new account), organize content and direct the user to specific pages on your corporate web site (searching for wealth management answers Joe, click on these links today), or gather additional information (fill out a short survey). All click activity can be tracked to the individual user making this an ideal tool for the sales savvy financial institution to respond to online activity in person. And nothing is MORE personal than that.

# QR Codes are Hot, Hot, Hot!

QR (quick response) codes compress contact information and offers into a two-dimensional graphic image. QR codes will boost client response to your advertising and direct marketing activity. And it is all trackable! If you have a smart phone (and who doesn't?) download a reader and take a picture of the image below. Here are six solid reasons to use QR codes:

- The road from prospect to message/offer just got shorter.

- Response tracking is super simple.

- Reach your clients & prospects now.

- Say more with less & get immediate sales conversions.

- QR codes are viral.

**You get dramatically higher response rates when you have convergent, multichannel Marketing—using direct mail, email, PURLs and QR codes all at once!**

# Understanding how to market to people NOT like YOU.

Did you know?

- The U.S. women's market is bigger than the total GDP of China and India, combined.

- Married couples with children make up fewer than 21% of all households.

- The number of folks who live alone, is now greater than 27% of the population.

- There are 102 million multicultural consumers in the U.S., with $3 trillion in buying power.

- Since 2000, 82% of U.S. population growth came from multicultural segments.

Kelly McDonald, in her book *How to Market to People Not Like You*, clearly articulates the power of values-based marketing. Ditch the demographics – marketing must reach out to people where they live – using their value system. This means that your financial institution must know your market, your clients and prospects, their priorities and what they care about. Touch their values and you'll touch their wallet.

You need to identify how your marketplace has become more diverse. Changing generational, ethnic and lifestyle segments within your community (and the unique values owned by each) require your understanding. How might this knowledge alter your marketing message?

# Taming the Social Media Shrew.

Is there profit in social media? Not yet. But there is definitely the potential for significant loss.

Social networking puts the power in the hands of the people. Your clients could be trashing your brand and you wouldn't know it. This is the risk of not engaging in social networking. Plugging in can help you manage this risk.

You can't not be there. Yet you must manage your expectations.

Social media (SM) isn't about getting. It is about giving and helping others. Those using SM just to get from others fail at SM. SM is about trust, and trust must be earned. Once lost, trust is hard to recover. In SM, there may be no second chance to recover.

# Final Thoughts

# Does your Marketing Stink?

Do you have expectations of marketing? Do you expect them to measure and prove a return on their marketing investment? Are you getting and leveraging strategic client intelligence? Is someone in marketing a part of your senior management team? Is marketing a partner at the table during your organization's strategic conversations? Is marketing driving qualified leads to your sales team? Are your marketing and sales teams aligned to optimize growth?

Marketing can no longer be "trinkets and trash," as many have expressed it. Your marketing cannot continue to do the same thing it has done and expect a different result. The world of banking is not the same today as it was even ten years ago.

## Your marketing cannot be the same.

# Isn't it time you got ma$$ive profit growth from your marketing?

Massive growth will not happen without a dramatic paradigm shift in what you expect from your marketing efforts. It all starts with getting valuable business intelligence, taking appropriate action, and then measuring the ROI of everything you do.

## As Jack Welch, former leader of GE stated, "Control your own destiny...or someone else will."

# "There is no try. There is only do, or do not."

— Yoda

# There are two kinds of marketing.

One that makes you
## *feel.*

And one that makes you
## *feel and act.*

One of these philosophies adds dollars to the bottom line. The other one is a giant black hole that can drain a budget in an instant. Your marketing must inspire your clients and prospects to **act**, not just feel.

## Now is the time for your marketing to deliver ma$$ive growth for your financial institution.

You can have success without making Marketing a partner in profit growth...but it is highly unlikely that you will get the massive growth you desire.

# What are you missing out on?

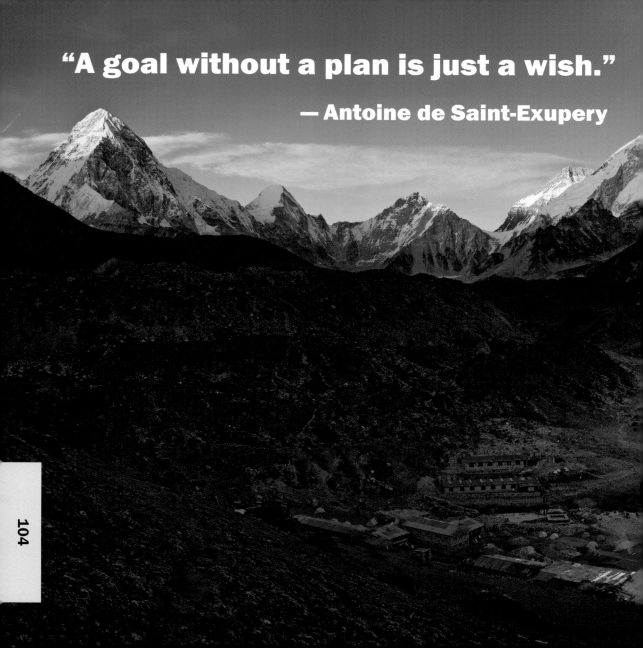

"A goal without a plan is just a wish."

— Antoine de Saint-Exupery

The trip to conquer Everest takes years of planning...the right equipment, the best counsel, plenty of money, personal conditioning, and perfect weather conditions. What obstacles will you face in achieving your goals? What is your plan?

# Acknowledgements:

There are many to thank. First let me start by thanking everyone at **MARQUIS**. I have never worked with a more inspiring group of caring and dedicated people.

I love books that make me think. I love simple turns of a phrase that bring unusual clarity to an otherwise complex idea. I love the poetry of a well placed verse. For any who have delivered on the promise of these ideas, my thanks and my complete amazement.

Thanks to **John & Jud** for their "vital" support of "smarketing!" And to **Jeff** for his help with many things, including JDC. **Julie**, they don't come better than you.

For the visual concept, layout and follow through, all thanks to **Charles Flemming**.

The whole idea of the book would likely still be only that…if not for **Tony Rizzo**. Thank you.

My thanks to **Noelle Smith** for sharing a book that revealed the inspiration for this one.

**Ron Buck**, thank you for sharing the wisdom of the "math of growth" with me.

**Robert Swafford**, **Joel Griffin**, **Todd Young**, **Sean Cunningham**, and **Mike Bartoo**…I thank you all for your industry insight, your feedback, and for your persnickety knowledge of grammar.

**To God be the glory.**

**About the author:** Jay Kassing has been writing about and for the financial services industry for over twenty years. President of MARQUIS, Jay lives in Dallas with his wife and five children. He can be reached at JayK@gomarquis.com.

*To see real life examples of how marketing can drive measurable results at financial institutions of all sizes, take a picture of the QR code on the right, using a QR reader from your smart phone. You can download a free QR Reader App.*

**It's about results.  Nothing else matters.**